Five-Star Meals
by Sue Frow

It's a lovely thing —everyone sitting down together, sharing food. So take a moment, before you dig in, to smile at your friends.

—Alice May Brock
American Cook and Restauranteur

This book is published by the Peoria Journal Star, Inc.
1 News Plaza
Peoria, Illinois 61643

ISBN: 0-9634793-5-0

Layout, design, and illustrations by Jean Slonneger

Production by TRC, Peoria, Illinois
Printed by Art and Print, Washington, Illinois

This book is printed on recycled Lynx opaque from Weyerhaeuser Paper Company.

A portion of the proceeds from the sale of this book will be donated to the Peoria Area Community Foundation for the funding of literacy programs.

~~~~~

My special thanks to Dennis Dimond, who first believed these columns had an audience, and to Janet Peterson and the staff of the Journal Star for making this book possible.

To Eric, Jean, and Ron,
who helped a column
become a book.

Introduction

Five-Star Meals is a collection of 24 dinner menus and their recipes which appeared in the *Journal Star* from May, 1991, through April, 1993.

I have added several new recipes in this book, as well as more detailed instructions, cook's tips, and some culinary humor. It's all served up with a generous number of drawings by my talented friend, Jean. These recipes have a seasonal theme. I believe that no strawberry should be served before its time—and in the Midwest, that usually means May.

Many were inspired by my travels, and they all reflect what I like to eat. French, Southwestern, and Caribbean cuisines are high on my list, so there is a liberal sprinkling of garlic and all kinds of peppers. You won't find even a reference to eggplant!

These recipes are not difficult, and most can be prepared for a busy weekday dinner. A few take longer and are suited to weekends or entertaining. Very little special equipment is required, other than some sharp knives, though a food processor expedites many procedures. My aim is to help you make the last meal of the day its most memorable one.

And what has happened to that meal in the 90's? Suddenly the dinner table has become a dangerous place. My earliest memories of this table were of enticing aromas and various textures and colors all coming together to tempt and then soothe me as hunger disappeared.

There were dinners at my grandmother's, who really did make the best pie crust in the whole world. We had crispy fried chicken, homemade rolls, and three vegetables (always). There was pecan pie or strawberry shortcake generously crowned with real whipped cream. They were satisfying dinners, ample and honest.

Why is this table now dangerous? In the 90's, there are insidious elements on it: fats, sodium, sugar, and additives. We're told that some are even life-threatening. We have been manipulated into avoiding them all, even if we are reasonably healthy. "Chicken Tonight" is more than a sauce brand—it's a mantra for avoiding red meat. Butter is banished, replaced by an airy spread with a countrified name and a long list of chemistry's magic. As for the whipped cream, its new substitute may be cool, but it is also waxy and cloying.

I believe an occasional steak and a spoonful of cream are small pleasures which do not endanger us; they make dinner enjoyable instead of endurable. And so I include them in my recipes. Centuries before the frenetic worry about fat, fiber, and LDLs, a Greek philosopher recommended all things in moderation.

And to that I add: It's Friday, so pass the butter and Bon Appetit!

★ CONTENTS ★

Notes

January

Cheese Straws

South of the Border
Soup

Mexican Cole Slaw

Fresh Pineapple

~ or ~

Linguine with Scallops
and Sun-Dried
Tomatoes

Spinach Salad with
Orange and Apple

Chocolate Surprise
Cupcakes

January always finds us seeking inner warmth, so choose a robust soup with Mexican spices and receive a double dose. Cheese straws are also slightly nippy, but the jicama and apple in the salad add a crisp, cool, temperate touch.

CHEESE STRAWS
4 dozen straws

1-1/2 teaspoons baking powder
1/4 teaspoon salt
1-1/4 cups flour
Cayenne pepper to taste—about 1/4 teaspoon
1 stick cold unsalted butter, in 8 slices
8 ounces sharp natural Cheddar cheese

1. Cut the cheese into 1/2-inch chunks. Place it in a food processor with the steel blade, and pulse to form coarse crumbs.

2. Sift the dry ingredients together, and add to the cheese along with the butter. Pulse until mixture is just coarser than cornmeal.

3. Dump the pastry onto a counter; pinch the dough together to form a solid mass. Press it into a rectangle and refrigerate it at least 30 minutes.

4. Roll 1/4-inch thick and cut with a ravioli cutter or knife into 4- x 3/4-inch rectangles. Re-roll the trimmings to make more straws.

5. Bake the straws at 400° on non-stick cookie sheets about 10 minutes, or until browned.

Note: These are best served warm. Store extras in a metal container. The dough freezes well for up to 3 months. Defrost it in the refrigerator overnight before baking.

SOUTH OF THE BORDER SOUP
About 8 Cups

1 cup dried pinto beans
1 pound boneless pork country-style ribs
1 tablespoon oil
1/2 cup each: chopped onion and celery
2 large cloves garlic, minced
1 can (14 ounces) whole tomatoes
1 teaspoon each: oregano, cumin seed, and
* crushed red pepper*
2 cups beef or chicken stock
4 cups water
2 cups sliced carrots
1 cup frozen baby lima beans
1 seven-ounce jar baby corn, rinsed and drained
Salt and pepper
2 tablespoons lime juice

Garnishes: *Minced fresh cilantro and sour*
* cream*

1. Rinse the beans, discarding any grit or any beans that are discolored. Cover by at least 3 inches with cool water and soak 8 hours. Rinse them again before proceeding.

2. Cut the meat into 1-inch cubes, trimming off fat. Heat the oil in a 3-quart soup pot and sear the meat until browned. Remove the meat and all but 1 tablespoon of the cooking fat.

Tip: To keep cilantro fresh, treat it like a bouquet and store it in the fridge in a glass of water. —S.F.

3. Lower the heat and cook the onion, celery, and garlic, stirring until soft, about 5 minutes.

4. Seed the tomatoes; add them with their liquid, the seasonings, stock, water, and the soaked beans.

5. Simmer about 1-1/2 hours, or until the beans and meat are almost done. Add the carrots, lima beans, and baby corn, and simmer a further 20 minutes.

6. Adjust the seasoning, adding the lime juice, and garnish with cilantro and sour cream.

Of soup and love, the first is best

—Spanish proverb

MEXICAN COLE SLAW
Serves 4

Dressing
3 tablespoons parsley, minced
2 teaspoons green onion, minced
2 tablespoons each: lemon juice and vinegar
1 teaspoon each: dry mustard and celery seed
Salt and pepper to taste

Salad
2 crisp red apples
1 small jícama (about 12 ounces)
2 small zucchini

1. Whisk the dressing ingredients; add salt and pepper to taste.

2. Quarter and core 1-1/2 apples and shred them, along with the jícama and zucchini. Blend with the dressing and refrigerate 30 minutes.

3. To serve, drain excess dressing, adjust seasoning, and garnish with thin slices of the remaining apple.

Please do not try this unless an adult is present!

New beginnings: Another year, and perhaps another attempt to modify our diets. If less red meat and more carbohydrate are in order, consider a seafood pasta. Balsamic vinegar and fresh fruit make the spinach salad appealingly light. Having been so virtuous, you are entitled to a chocolate cupcake with a cheesecake filling (just one).

SPINACH SALAD WITH ORANGE AND APPLE
Serves 4

Salad
6 cups fresh spinach, cleaned, stems removed
1 orange
1 red apple
A few paper-thin rings of red onion
1/2 cup hazelnuts or almonds for garnish
Balsamic Dressing to taste

Dressing (makes about 2/3 cup)
2 tablespoons balsamic vinegar
8 tablespoons good-quality olive oil
Salt and freshly ground pepper

1. Make the dressing by whisking together the vinegar, oil, and salt and pepper to taste.

2. With a vegetable peeler, remove several thin strips of rind from the orange. Finely mince them and add 2 teaspoons to the dressing.

3. Toast the nuts in a 325° oven for 8 to 10 minutes, or until they are fragrant. For hazelnuts, wrap immediately in a towel and rub them to remove most of the papery brown skin. Cool the nuts and chop them coarsely.

4. Peel and section the orange and cube the apple. Add, with the onion rings, to the spinach.

5. To serve, toss with just enough dressing to moisten and garnish with the toasted nuts.

Tip: Use fruit juices, chicken stock, or juices left from roasting meat to replace some of the oil in dressings; they are good flavor enhancers. —S.F.

LINGUINE WITH SCALLOPS AND SUN-DRIED TOMATOES
Serves 4

1 cup fresh mushrooms
2 tablespoons lemon juice
1 tablespoon butter
3/4 cup sun-dried tomato halves (not oil-packed)
2 tablespoons olive oil
1/4 cup sliced green onion
1 pound bay scallops
2 tablespoons flour
1 cup frozen peas
1 tablespoon minced lemon peel (yellow part only)
1/2 cup chicken stock
1/2 cup minced parsley
Salt and pepper to taste
Optional: 1 teaspoon thyme leaves
~~~~~
8 ounces linguine

1. Clean the mushrooms and cut them into quarters. Place the mushrooms in a small saucepan with the butter and 1 tablespoon of the lemon juice; cover and bring to a boil. Set aside.

2. Pour boiling water over the tomatoes and let them stand three minutes. Drain, pat dry, and cut them into pieces.

3. In a large sauté pan, heat the olive oil over moderately high heat and add the green onion; sauté until soft.

4. Place the scallops in a sieve and rinse them with cool water; pat dry. Shake flour over them to coat lightly. Sauté with the onion, peas, lemon peel, and optional thyme until just done, about 2 minutes.

5. Add all remaining ingredients and cook until slightly thickened, another minute. Season to taste and serve over hot cooked linguine.

CHOCOLATE SURPRISE CUPCAKES
About 30

Batter
3 cups flour
2 cups sugar
1/2 cup unsweetened cocoa
2 teaspoons baking soda
1 teaspoon salt
2 large eggs
1-1/2 cups cold water
2/3 cup oil
2 tablespoons vinegar
2 teaspoons pure vanilla extract

Filling
8 ounces cream cheese
1 tablespoon flour
1/3 cup sugar
1 large egg
1 cup mini chocolate chips

1. Preheat the oven to 375° and line 2 -3/4-inch muffin pans with paper liners.
2. Make the filling by softening the cream cheese and beating the sugar and flour into it. Add the egg and beat until smooth. Fold in the chocolate chips.
3. For the cupcakes, sift the dry ingredients into a large bowl. Whisk together

the remaining ingredients and add to flour mixture, beating just until smooth.

4. Half fill the cupcake tins with batter; top each with 2 teaspoons cheese mixture, and then distribute the remaining batter on top.

5. Bake the cupcakes 20 to 25 minutes. If you wish, sift powdered sugar over tops, or drizzle with chocolate glaze.

Note: This large quantity can be halved. For the filling, beat the egg and use only 2 tablespoons of it.

If you have low standards and no patience for details, better send out for pizza.

—Tom Wicker
American journalist and author

February

Pear and Blue Cheese
Salad

Roast Lamb with an
Herbed Crust

Carrots with Orange
and Ginger

Meringue with Lemon
Cream

~ or ~

A New "Garden"
Salad

Chicken in Mustard
Cream

Zucchini with Basil

French Bread

Jubilant Cherries

The way to charm your Valentine lies through the kitchen. Aromas of herbs on roast lamb and orange-ginger carrots should capture some attention. A good salad partner is sliced ripe pears and crumbled blue cheese on romaine lettuce, sprinkled with a classic vinaigrette. But the spotlight is on dessert: an almond meringue filled with lemon cream. Heartfelt praise for the cook!

PEAR AND BLUE CHEESE SALAD
Serves 4

Salad
3 ripe winter pears (Bosc or Anjou)
6 tablespoons crumbled Danish blue cheese
4 cups chopped or sliced romaine lettuce

Dressing
2 tablespoons red-wine or balsamic vinegar
2 teaspoons Dijon mustard
Salt and pepper to taste
6 tablespoons oil (olive oil and salad oil
    combined)

1. Make the vinaigrette by whisking the vinegar, mustard, salt and pepper. Add the oil in a stream, whisking. Adjust seasoning.

2. Line the plates with the romaine. Peel the pears if desired; core them and cut into crescents. Arrange the pears on the lettuce, top with cheese, and sprinkle with the dressing.

ROAST LAMB WITH AN HERBED CRUST
Serves 6

*3-1/2 pounds leg of lamb (from sirloin end),
  boned
1/2 cup fresh French bread crumbs
1/2 cup grated Parmesan cheese
1-1/2 tablespoons minced fresh rosemary (or 2
  teaspoons dried, crumbled)
3 tablespoons minced fresh parsley
1 large clove garlic, minced
2 tablespoons olive oil
1-1/2 tablespoons Dijon mustard
Salt and freshly ground pepper to taste*

1. Remove all fat and silvery membrane from the meat. Tie it twice to make a compact roast.

2. Make the crust by combining the bread crumbs, cheese, herbs, minced garlic, and one tablespoon of the oil.

3. Coat the underside of the lamb with the remaining oil and season lightly with salt and pepper. Sprinkle more pepper on the top side, then coat this surface with mustard. Press the crumb mixture firmly over the top and sides to make a thick layer.

4. Preheat the oven to 450° and roast the lamb 15 minutes. Reduce the heat to 375° and roast about 30 minutes more, or until a thermometer reads 130° (this is medium rare, or rosy inside; add about 10 minutes for medium).

5. Let the roast stand 15 minutes at room temperature before carving.

CARROTS WITH ORANGE AND GINGER
Serves 4

1 pound tender young carrots
1/2 cup each: fresh orange juice and water
2 teaspoons butter
1/2 teaspoon ginger
Salt to taste
3 tablespoons minced fresh cilantro

1. Peel the carrots and place them in a small saucepan along with all other ingredients, except the cilantro. Cover, bring to a boil, and simmer them about 20 minutes, or until just tender.

2. Remove the carrots and rapidly boil down the liquid until about 1/2 cup remains. Swirl the carrots in the glaze and sprinkle them with the cilantro.

Tip: Buy garlic heads that are tightly closed — like an onion — and store them uncovered in a dry, dark spot. —S.F.

MERINGUE WITH LEMON CREAM
Serves 6-8

Lemon Filling (*Makes 1-1/4 cups*)
2 large lemons
1/2 cup sugar
3 egg yolks
pinch salt
6 tablespoons unsalted butter, melted

Meringue
6 large egg whites, room temperature
Pinch each: cream of tartar and salt
1-1/2 cups sugar
2 teaspoons vanilla extract
1/4 teaspoon almond extract
8 tablespoons ground almonds or pecans
Butter and flour to coat the pie pan
~~~~~
1/2 cup heavy cream

Garnish: Lemon slices and additional whipped
cream

    1. Remove the peel (yellow part only) of one lemon and chop it coarsely. Squeeze the lemons to yield 1/3 cup juice; reserve. In a processor, combine the peel with the sugar and process until finely grated. Add the egg yolks, salt, and lemon juice, blending just to mix.
    2. Pour the mixture into a heavy saucepan and whisk in the butter. Cook, stirring,

over medium heat until thickened, 5 to 10 minutes. Refrigerate the filling until cold.

3. Preheat the oven to 300°; butter and flour a 9-inch pie pan. Beat the egg whites until foamy; add cream of tartar and salt, beating until soft peaks form. Slowly add the sugar, then the flavoring, beating until the peaks are stiff and glossy.

4. Fold in the nuts and fill the pan, making a rim on the sides. Bake the meringue until firm and light gold, about 60 to 70 minutes. Cool and store air-tight.

5. Beat the cream until thick, not stiff. Fold into 1 cup of the lemon mixture and pour into the meringue. Refrigerate at least 2 hours, or overnight. Garnish with lemon slices and cream.

The hen is an egg's way of producing another egg.

—Samuel Butler
English novelist and essayist

A second dinner designed for February is partly patriotic, with cherries for Washington, and vaguely Valentine: the love apple, or tomato, appears in the salad and in the sauce for the chicken.

A NEW "GARDEN" SALAD
Serves 4

Dressing (Makes 1 cup)
4 tablespoons fresh lime juice, or white or red-
    wine vinegar
2 teaspoons Dijon mustard
2/3 cup salad oil
Salt and freshly ground pepper to taste
Optional: 1 teaspoon honey or sugar

Salad
3 large navel oranges
2 medium tomatoes (or 6 plum tomatoes)
2 California avocadoes, ripe but firm
8 large fresh mushrooms
Greens to serve the salad: Red leaf or
    watercress (About 3 cups)

1. Whisk the lime juice or vinegar with the mustard. Slowly add the oil in a stream, whisking. Season to taste with salt and pepper; add honey if you wish.

March

Mixed Green Salad
with Parmesan

Salmon on a Bed of
Leeks

Herbed Rice

Oranges a l'Orange

~ or ~

Cucumber and Mint
Salad

Thai-Style Noodles

Sparkling Fruit

When it is almost Spring, dinner could easily be poached fish fillets with some light, bright vegetables. This is a colorful menu, especially if you choose salmon. If you wish, shave some Parmesan over the salad, or use bits of blue cheese. Oranges with orange liqueur provide a simple, refreshing finale.

SALMON ON A BED OF LEEKS
Serves 4

4 salmon fillets, about 6 to 8 ounces each
2 medium leeks, cleaned and trimmed
2 carrots, peeled
1 sweet red pepper, halved, seeded, and the ribs
*   removed*
1 tablespoon each: butter and oil
1/4 cup chicken stock
Salt and pepper to taste
1 tablespoon minced fresh dill, or 1-1/2
*   teaspoons dried*
Drops of fresh lemon juice

1. Rinse the salmon and pat it dry.
2. Cut the leeks lengthwise into halves, and then cut the halves into quarters. Rinse them very well under cold water to remove any grit.

Slice the white and medium-green part into 1-1/2-inch lengths, discarding the tough, darker green top portion. Cut each section lengthwise into matchstick pieces. Cut the carrot and red pepper into pieces that are the same size as the leek.

    3. Melt the butter and oil in a non-stick frying pan just large enough to hold the fish. Sauté the vegetables over medium heat, stirring, just until soft—about 5 minutes. Add the stock and lower the heat so that the liquid simmers.

    4. Place the fish on top and sprinkle it with salt, pepper, dill, and drops of lemon juice. Cover and steam for about 10 minutes, or until fish is just opaque. Serve each fillet on a bed of the vegetables.

    Note: Try cod, halibut, or orange roughy instead of salmon.

HERBED RICE
Serves 4

1/2 cup wild rice
1/2 cup brown rice
1 tablespoon oil
1 tablespoon butter
1/4 cup chopped green or yellow onion
2 cups chicken stock
1 teaspoon thyme leaves
1/2 cup minced fresh parsley, preferably Italian
Salt and freshly ground pepper to taste

1. Rinse the wild rice well with cold water and drain it. Melt the butter and oil in a heavy 1-quart saucepan. Sauté the onion for 2 or 3 minutes, or until soft. Add both wild and brown rice and cook, stirring, to coat the rice with the onion mixture.

2. Add the thyme, parsley, pepper, and chicken stock and bring to the simmer. Stir once, cover, and reduce heat to low. Cook about 45 minutes, or until the liquid is absorbed. Adjust seasoning, adding salt if needed.

Note: Experiment with this basic recipe. All brown rice or all wild rice can be used; all brown rice will cook slightly faster than the mixture. Try an aromatic rice such as Basmati or Texmati. A handful of sliced fresh mushrooms can be sautéed with the onion. Toasted nuts, especially almonds or pecans, can

be stirred in at the end. Raisins, currants, or
sliced dried apricots can be cooked with the
rice. This is a very friendly complement to pork,
chicken, or turkey. Leftover rice freezes well.

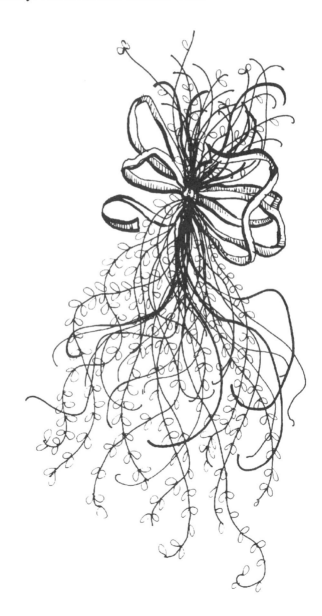

ORANGES A L'ORANGE
Serves 4

4 large navel oranges
1/3 cup sugar
1/2 cup water
2 tablespoons orange liqueur, such as Grand
  Marnier or Cointreau

1. Peel the oranges, removing just the colored skin with a vegetable peeler. Reserve the peel from 2 oranges. Use a serrated or very sharp knife to peel all the fruit, removing the white pith and membrane.
2. Slice the oranges crosswise into 1/2-inch slices, saving any juice. Arrange them in an attractive bowl. Sprinkle with the liqueur and reserved juices and refrigerate for up to 6 hours.
3. Stack two or three strips of reserved peel, colored side down, and cut them into very thin lengthwise pieces with a sharp knife. Repeat with the other strips.
4. Bring the sugar and water to a boil and boil slowly 3 minutes. Add the strips of peel and cook them, stirring, about 5 minutes, or until they become translucent. Remove from heat and cool them in the syrup. At serving time, drain the julienne and arrange it over the orange slices.

Note: In the summertime, substitute a sauce of fresh puréed strawberries or raspberries for the julienne.

Cutting fruits and vegetables into julienne

① Use a vegetable peeler to remove just the colored rind of an orange or lemon. Aim for long, straight strips.

②

Make a stack of no more than three strips and place them shiny side down. Keeping the knife tip on the board, cut matchstick-like pieces, rotating the knife slightly after each cut. For vegetables, be sure the slices are an even thickness before beginning the julienne cut.

No chance for a warming mid-winter getaway? This Thai-inspired entree will bring a little heat as well as exotic flavors to your dinner table. The salad and fruit dessert provide a nice balance. No frequent-flyer miles will be awarded, but there is a bonus: a low-fat dinner that can be vegetarian.

CUCUMBER AND MINT SALAD
Serves 4

1 medium cucumber
Salt (a scant 1/2 teaspoon)
2 plum tomatoes
1 tablespoon chopped fresh mint leaves (or 2
  teaspoons dried, crumbled)
1 tablespoon minced green onion
3/4 cup plain yogurt
Sugar and lemon juice to taste —1 or 2
  teaspoons each

1. Halve the cucumber lengthwise and remove the seeds. Cut it into crosswise slices, about 1/4 inch thick. Sprinkle the cucumber lightly with salt and set aside for 10 minutes.

2. Halve the tomatoes, remove the seeds, and chop them. Press any moisture from the cucumbers and combine them lightly with the tomatoes and remaining ingredients.

3 Adjust seasoning. Serve the salad as a condiment with Thai-style noodles.

THAI-STYLE NOODLES
Serves 4

4 ounces rice noodles (also called rice stick)
2 large stalks lemongrass (or 1 tablespoon
  grated lemon rind)
1 one-inch piece fresh ginger
1/2 cup dry-roasted peanuts
1 cup (packed) fresh cilantro leaves
2 large cloves garlic, peeled
1 jalapeño pepper, seeds and ribs removed
~~~~~
1 large carrot
1 medium zucchini
1 cup pea pods, tips removed
1 small red pepper
4 green onions
~~~~~
1 tablespoon Kikkoman light soy sauce
2 tablespoons lime juice
1 tablespoon tomato paste
2 teaspoons each: anchovy paste and sugar
1/4 cup chicken stock
About 2 tablespoons peanut oil
1 egg, lightly beaten

Garnish: *Lime wedges and cilantro leaves*

Optional: *Grilled shrimp, chicken, or steak*
  strips

1. Cover the rice noodles with hot water; soak them for 10 minutes. Drain well and cut them with scissors into shorter lengths.

2. Prepare all vegetables before proceeding, as the cooking goes quickly. Remove the outer leaves of the lemongrass; cut the bottom 3-inch lower core into 3 pieces and discard the rest. Peel the ginger; cut it in half.

3. Using a processor, coarsely chop the peanuts. Remove them and set aside. With the processor running, add lemongrass, garlic, ginger, cilantro, and jalapeño; stop when all is finely minced.

4. Peel the carrot and cut it into 1-inch chunks. Add them to the processor and chop coarsely. Halve the zucchini and cut it into quarter slices. Cut the peapods and red pepper into strips. Slice the green onions, including tops.

5. Make the sauce by mixing the soy, lime, tomato, anchovy paste, sugar, and stock.

6. Heat a large non-stick skillet or wok to medium high; add the peanut oil and stir fry all vegetables and the lemongrass mixture until almost tender; then add the rice noodles, peanuts, the egg, and sauce ingredients. Stir-fry one or two minutes, or until hot. Adjust seasoning.

7. Garnish and serve the optional ingredients alongside.

Note: There is a real workout for the kitchen knife here, but all the vegetables can be prepared ahead and refrigerated. Linguine may be substituted for rice noodles. Cook it, rinse with cool water, and drain; add the pasta during the final stir-fry.

Tip: Peel fresh ginger, cut into chunks, and cover with dry sherry or vodka. Keeps refrigerated at least a month. —S.F.

SPARKLING FRUIT
Serves 4

4 cups fresh fruit: oranges, strawberries,
  peaches, or grapes
2 cups champagne or Asti Spumante
2 tablespoons honey, or to taste
1 teaspoon minced orange rind
Fresh mint for garnish

1. Choose a combination of the best seasonal fruit. Cut it into slices or chunks and place in individual bowls.
2. To serve, gently stir together the champagne, honey, and orange rind. Pour it over the fruit and garnish with a mint sprig, if desired.

April

Asparagus Mimosa

Veal Rolls with Lemon
Stuffing

Carrots and Green
Beans with Dill

Almond Tuile Cookies

~ or ~

Spring Vegetable Soup

Asparagus Frittata

Strawberry-Rhubarb
Crisp

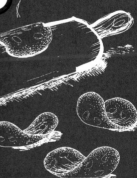

Here comes the sun, so this April dinner has Spring colors and the freshness of lemon and orange throughout. Begin with a cold asparagus salad, and accompany the veal rolls with steamed carrots and green beans tossed with dill butter. The almond cookies are curved like French roof tiles, or tuiles. Serve them with ice cream or fruit, or dip one end in melted chocolate to complement after-dinner coffee.

ASPARAGUS MIMOSA
Serves 4

1-1/2 pounds fresh asparagus
2 tablespoons white or red-wine vinegar
6 tablespoons oil—include some olive oil
2 teaspoons finely minced shallot or white of
  green onion
Salt and pepper to taste
1 hard-boiled egg
1/2 cup minced parsley

Some of Spring's favorite flavors are featured here. The soup, with leeks, spinach, and peas, is truly "spring green." Asparagus becomes a light entree that would be equally nice for brunch. And strawberries and rhubarb are perfectly paired in a simple fruit crisp.

SPRING VEGETABLE SOUP
Serves 6

2 medium leeks
2 tablespoons butter
3 tablespoons flour
2 ribs celery, chopped
1-1/2 quarts well-flavored chicken stock
1 teaspoon thyme leaves, or 1 tablespoon
  chopped fresh dill
Salt and pepper to taste
1 cup frozen peas (or small fresh peas)
1 quart (packed) shredded spinach leaves
Optional: 1 cup diced new potatoes

1. Trim the root end of the leeks; slash them lengthwise, and rinse them very well to remove sand and grit. Chop the white and tender green part.

2. Melt the butter in a large saucepan and add the chopped leek. Cook over medium heat, stirring, until coated with butter. Add the flour and cook, continuing to stir, until bubbly.

3. Now add the celery, stock, herb flavoring, peas, and optional potatoes; simmer 15 minutes, or until the vegetables are tender.

4. Add the spinach and simmer another 5 minutes. Adjust seasoning and serve.

Note: This soup may be enriched with cream, or puréed and served cold, garnished with sour cream or yogurt.

ASPARAGUS FRITTATA
Serves 4

12 ounces asparagus
1 tablespoon butter, melted
Salt, freshly ground pepper, and nutmeg to taste
1 teaspoon lemon juice
1/2 cup diced Jarlsberg Swiss cheese
1/2 cup chopped prosciutto (or Canadian
    bacon)
1/2 cup sliced mushrooms
2 tablespoons each: chopped parsley and
    minced green onion
4 large eggs
1/4 cup grated Parmesan cheese

1. Wash and trim the asparagus. Remove the butt end and peel the stalks. Cut the

asparagus into one-inch pieces on the diagonal. Blanch them in plenty of boiling water until barely tender; pat dry.

2. Spray a 10 or 11-inch pie pan or quiche pan with nonstick spray and preheat the oven to 350°.

3. Toss the asparagus with the butter and season it with salt, pepper, a pinch of nutmeg, and the lemon juice. Place it in the prepared pan, and sprinkle the Jarlsberg, prosciutto, mushrooms, parsley and green onion on top.

4. Lightly whisk the eggs with a pinch of salt and pour over. Sprinkle with Parmesan. Bake the frittata about 30 minutes, or until eggs are set and lightly browned.

5. If some liquid remains, run the frittata under the broiler for a minute or two. Serve in wedges.

STRAWBERRY-RHUBARB CRISP
Serves 4

2 cups sliced rhubarb (cut in 1/2-inch pieces)
1-1/2 cups strawberry halves
2 teaspoons minced orange peel
2 tablespoons orange juice
1/3 cup sugar
2 teaspoons cornstarch
~~~~~
1/4 cup each: regular oatmeal and flour
1/3 cup sugar
1/4 teaspoon nutmeg
3 tablespoons butter

1. Combine the strawberries, rhubarb, orange peel, and juice.
2. Mix the sugar and cornstarch; stir gently into the fruit and place the mixture in a 1-quart baking dish sprayed with non-stick spray.
3. Stir the dry ingredients together and cut butter in until the topping is like cornmeal. Sprinkle over the fruit.
4. Bake at 375° for 40 minutes, or until browned and bubbly. Serve warm.

Tip: Dump strawberries and all berries onto a paper-towel lined pan; store them unwashed in a single layer in the refrigerator. Keeps one wet berry from creating mischief. —S.F.

May

Chicken and Shrimp
Skewers

New Potatoes with
Lemon and Parsley

Green Bean and Walnut
Salad

Strawberry Souffle Roll

~ or ~

Cornish Hens with
Chutney Glaze

Asparagus Stir-Fry

Peas and Yellow Rice

Strawberries in a
Snowbank

Here is a dinner for late spring, when the grill is asking to be used. Fresh pineapple and sweet red peppers make the skewers colorful. Easy accompaniments are little butter-browned potatoes and a vegetable salad with a tarragon vinaigrette. The strawberry dessert is pure elegance—watch it disappear!

CHICKEN AND SHRIMP SKEWERS
Serves 4

Skewers
4 boneless skinless chicken breast halves
12 large shrimp, peeled and deveined
1/4 fresh ripe pineapple
1 small sweet red pepper

Basting Sauce
2/3 cup hot pepper jelly
2 tablespoons Dijon mustard
2 tablespoons lemon or lime juice
2 tablespoons oil
Salt to taste

1. Cut the breast halves into 3 or 4 lengthwise strips, each about an inch wide.

GREEN BEAN AND WALNUT SALAD
Serves 4

Tarragon dressing *(1 cup)*
4 tablespoons red or white-wine vinegar
2 teaspoons Dijon mustard
1 small clove garlic, minced
1 tablespoon fresh tarragon leaves, chopped,
  or 1 teaspoon dried
Salt and freshly ground pepper to taste
3/4 cup oil (part olive oil if desired)

Salad
1-1/2 pounds small green beans
1 cup walnut halves or pieces
8 cherry or plum tomatoes, halved
1 small head Boston or red leaf lettuce

1. Make the dressing by whisking the vinegar, mustard, garlic, tarragon, salt, and pepper. Slowly add the oil, whisking. Adjust seasoning.

2. Trim the ends of the beans and cook them in a large quantity of boiling salted water until barely tender. Drain them and refresh in cold water. Pat them dry.

3. Toast the walnuts in a 325° oven for about 8 minutes, or until they are fragrant.

1. Preheat the oven to 350°. Rinse the hens and discard the giblets. Pat them dry and place them in a shallow roasting pan. Quarter the onion and place a piece inside each hen.

2. Melt the butter; add the curry powder and use this to coat the hens. Bake 30 minutes. Combine the remaining ingredients and glaze the hens.

3. Bake an additional 30 minutes, or until the internal temperature is 165°, basting several times with the pan juices.

4. When the hens are done, skim any fat from the glaze and reduce until syrupy. Pour over the hens and garnish with fresh fruit.

Tip: To cut pineapple wedges easily, twist off the frond and cut fruit into quarters. Use a grapefruit knife to remove flesh from rind. Trim off core. —S.F.

Tip: To store asparagus, trim the butt end and stand it upright in a container. Add a few inches of cool water, cover loosely, and refrigerate.—S.F.

ASPARAGUS STIR-FRY
Serves 4

1-1/2 pounds asparagus—thin spears are best
2 green onions
2 tablespoons oil
1 teaspoon chicken stock granules
Pinch of sugar
1 teaspoon grated lemon rind
1 tablespoon lemon juice
4 tablespoons toasted slivered almonds

1. Wash and trim the asparagus. Slice it diagonally into 1-inch pieces. If you use thicker asparagus, peel the stalks. Thinly slice the green onion.

2. Toast the almonds in a 325° oven about 5 minutes, or until fragrant.

3. Heat the oil in a wok or frying pan until very hot, and then add the onion and asparagus. Stir-fry until just tender—about 4 minutes. Season with stock, sugar, and the lemon.

4. Sprinkle the asparagus with the almonds and serve immediately.

PEAS AND YELLOW RICE
Serves 4

1 tablespoon butter
1 cup white rice
2 cups hot chicken stock
1 teaspoon turmeric
1 cup frozen peas, slightly defrosted
Salt and pepper to taste

1. Melt the butter in a small saucepan and add the rice, stirring to coat it well.
2. Add the stock and turmeric. Bring to a boil, stir once, and cover.
3. Simmer 15 minutes. Uncover and add the peas.
4. Remove the rice from the heat and let stand 5 minutes. Uncover, stir gently, and adjust seasoning.

STRAWBERRIES IN A SNOWBANK
Serves 4

1 quart strawberries
2 tablespoons each: orange juice and honey
1/2 cup whipping cream
2 tablespoons powdered sugar
2 teaspoons vanilla
4 tablespoons sweetened shredded coconut
2 tablespoons minced fresh mint

1. Wash the strawberries gently and remove their hulls. Pat them dry. Cut the berries in half and sweeten to taste with orange juice and honey. Refrigerate.

2. Add the powdered sugar and vanilla to the cream and whip it until it forms soft peaks.

3. To serve, place the berries in individual dishes; top with cream and sprinkle with the coconut and mint. The dessert is especially attractive layered in parfait glasses

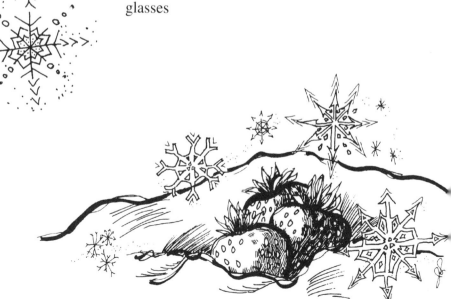

Note: Berries and cream may be prepared up to 4 hours in advance and refrigerated separately. If you wish to whip the cream ahead of time, when it reaches the consistency you like, place it in a sieve set over a bowl in the refrigerator. This will let excess moisture drip through, and the cream will keep its shape and not separate.

It isn't so much what's on the table that matters, as what's on the chairs.

—W.S. Gilbert
English author and librettist

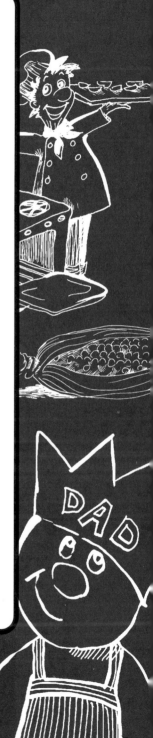

June

Salad of Summer Greens

Mediterranean Flank Steak

New "Fries"

French Apple Tart

~ or ~

A Caesar for the '90s

Grilled Pork Caribbean

Grilled or Boiled Corn on the Cob

Bittersweet Chocolate Pecan Cake

The quintessential Father's Day dinner must be steak, potatoes, and apple pie. Here is an easy way to give Dad what he wants. Flank steak is an inexpensive, lean and tasty alternative to rib-eye or a T-bone. No deep-fryer is required for the potatoes—oven-roast them for a crisp result. The French tart is glamorous with an apricot glaze, and not at all difficult to make.

MEDITERRANEAN FLANK STEAK
SERVES 4-6

1 flank steak, about 1-1/2 pounds
1 large clove garlic
3 tablespoons olive oil
2 teaspoons paprika
Salt and freshly ground pepper to taste

1. Crush the garlic and combine it with the olive oil, paprika, and freshly ground pepper to taste. Remove any fat or tissue from the steak and score it lightly on the surface, using a sharp knife.

2. Preheat the oven to 400°. Select a heavy pan just large enough to hold the potatoes in a single layer. Add just enough oil to cover the bottom of the pan.

3. Peel and split the garlic, and add to the pan along with the potatoes. Toss to coat them; sprinkle with salt and pepper. Bake 35 to 40 minutes, stirring occasionally, until brown.

Note: Vary this recipe by using new red-skinned potatoes; cutting them differently (slices or halves); or adding herbs to the oil, such as thyme or rosemary. These have lots of crunch with much less oil than french fries!

FRENCH APPLE TART
Serves 6-8

1 sheet frozen puff pastry (Pepperidge Farm),
*   defrosted*
Flour
3 large Golden Delicious apples
1 tablespoon lemon juice
3 tablespoons sugar
~~~~~
One 12-ounce jar apricot preserves

1. Preheat the oven to 450°. On a very lightly floured surface, roll the pastry to a 15- x 10-inch rectangle. Place it on an ungreased heavy, rimmed baking sheet and refrigerate while preparing the apples.

2. Peel and quarter the apples; slice them into even slices a scant 1/4-inch thick. Toss with the lemon juice. Arrange the slices in overlapping rows to completely cover the pastry. Sprinkle with the sugar.

3. Bake 15 to 20 minutes, or until the apples are tender and pastry is browned. Cool 15 minutes before glazing.

4. To glaze the tart, press the preserves through a fine sieve to remove fruit pieces. Bring the glaze to boil; while it is very hot, apply it with a soft brush to the entire surface of the tart.

5. Serve the tart warm or at room temperature, preferably within a few hours of baking.

Tip: Both Granny Smith and Golden Delicious apples are year-round winners. Take a bite of either one, and use both for pies and applesauce. —S.F.

Variation: To make a strawberry tart, prick the pastry all over and bake it until browned, about 15 minutes. Let cool. Melt currant jelly and lightly brush the surface of the pastry. Lay halved strawberries over the top and brush again with melted jelly.

Another menu which will please Dad as much as a below-par golf score is this one. The updated Caesar salad has authentic taste but no undercooked eggs. Try the piquant pork basting sauce on chicken, seafood, and fish such as snapper and yellowfin tuna.

A "CAESAR" FOR THE 90'S
Serves 4

Caesar Dressing *(Makes about 1-1/2 cups)*
1/4 cup mayonnaise
1/2 cup lemon juice
2 teaspoons anchovy paste
3/4 cup oil
1 clove garlic, crushed
1/2 cup freshly grated Parmesan cheese
Freshly ground pepper to taste

Salad
6 cups total: Assorted salad greens, pepper
*   strips, and sweet Vidalia onion rings*
1 cup croutons from rye or whole-wheat bread
1/2 cup Parmesan cheese for garnish

1. Make the dressing by whisking together the mayonnaise, lemon juice and anchovy paste. Whisk in the oil, then add the garlic and Parmesan.

2. Choose a mixture of torn romaine lettuce and radicchio leaves for the salad, including some red and yellow pepper strips and the onion rings.

3. Toss the greens with just enough dressing to moisten, and garnish with the Parmesan and croutons.

GRILLED PORK CARIBBEAN
Serves 4

4 butterfly pork chops, one inch thick
2 large juicy limes
6 small green onions, trimmed
1 clove garlic
2 tablespoons parsley, chopped
1 or 2 hot peppers (jalapeño or West Indies
"bonnet")
Pinch of thyme leaves
4 tablespoons oil
Salt and pepper to taste

1. Squeeze the limes to yield 6 tablespoons of juice. Mince the onions and garlic; combine with the parsley and lime juice.

2. Wear rubber gloves to mince the peppers. Discard the seeds and ribs unless you like an extra-hot sauce. Add the peppers, thyme and oil to the lime mixture and season to taste with salt and pepper.

3. Brush the chops lightly with the sauce before grilling—about 4 minutes per side over medium-hot coals. Baste liberally with more sauce before serving.

Tip: After mincing garlic, rub fingers with salt, and then wash them with cool water and soap. —S.F.

HONEY AND HERB BASTE
About 1 cup

1/2 cup oil
1/3 cup rice-wine or cider vinegar
1/4 cup honey
1 clove garlic, minced
1 teaspoon each: paprika, dry mustard, thyme,
  and marjoram
Salt and freshly ground pepper to taste

Whisk together all ingredients. A natural with
chicken or pork.

MEXICAN SANGRITA BASTE
About 1-1/3 cups

1/2 cup each: tomato juice and orange juice
2 tablespoons lime juice
1 tablespoon minced onion
1 small jalapeno pepper, seeded and minced
3 tablespoons oil
Salt to taste

Whisk together all ingredients. Use this sauce to
marinate seafood, tuna, pork, or chicken 30
minutes before grilling. Brush with additional
sauce as you cook.

Tip: It's a fish fact: no matter how you cook it, count on ten minutes per inch, measured at the thickest part. —S.F.

HERBED SUMMER SQUASH
Serves 2 to 4

2 small zucchini or yellow squash—each no
  more than 6 inches long
1-1/2 tablespoons butter or margarine
2 green onions, minced
1 tablespoon each: minced fresh basil or dill
2 tablespoons minced parsley
2 tablespoons each: fresh breadcrumbs and
  grated Parmesan cheese
Salt and pepper to taste

1. Cut the squash in half lengthwise and scoop out the center pulp, reserving it. Invert the shells onto paper towels while you make the filling.

2. Chop the pulp and then sauté it, with the onion, in 1/2 tablespoon butter until soft. Season to taste with the basil or dill, salt, and pepper. Fill the squash shells with the mixture.

3. Melt the remaining butter and combine it with the parsley, breadcrumbs, and cheese. Sprinkle the crumb mixture over the squash.

4. Bake the shells in a 400° oven about 20 minutes, or until tender and browned.

Note: The squash can be prepared several hours ahead and refrigerated.

mill to remove the seeds. Sweeten to taste and refrigerate.

    4. To serve, roll the ice cream in the nuts and place each scoop between two peach halves. Pour the raspberry sauce over the dessert.

Tip: Peaches and tomatoes can both be peeled in a snap by pouring boiling water over them. Let stand about 30 seconds, then rinse with cool water. The skins will slip off easily. —S.F.

What is sauce for the goose may be sauce for the gander but is not necessarily sauce for the chicken, the duck, the turkey or the guinea hen.

—Alice B. Toklas,
American writer

Greek flavors—lamb, tomatoes, spinach and especially mint—inspired this menu. The chutney and orzo also complement chicken. Add a marinated cucumber salad if you wish, but be sure to save room for a cool chocolate dessert. The mint cream makes it super, but so would a few raspberries.

GREEK LAMB PATTIES
Serves 4

*1-1/2 pounds lean ground lamb (or
  ground chuck)*
2 egg whites
2 tablespoons minced fresh mint
1/4 cup minced green onion
*1/2 teaspoon each: cinnamon and
  ground cumin*
*Salt and freshly ground pepper to
  taste*

1. Stir together the egg whites, mint, green onion, and spices. Combine lightly with the

September

A Presidential Salad

Cajun Catfish

Corn and Cheddar
Pudding

Fresh Plum and Ginger
Tart

~ or ~

Couscous Salad

Moroccan-Style Fish

Spicy Fresh Fruit

Butter Cookies

Spicy seasonings for September's cooler days, and a chance to use fresh produce one more time. The salad features broccoli, the targeted vegetable of George Bush. Serve it with zippy fish fillets and a wonderful fresh fruit tart.

CAJUN CATFISH
Serves 4

4 six-ounce catfish fillets, 1/2 inch thick
1-1/2 cups fine bread crumbs (use French or
*   Italian bread)*
3/4 cup finely chopped pecans
1/2 teaspoon each: cayenne and salt
1-1/2 tablespoons Creole or Dijon mustard
3/4 cup milk
Oil for frying—about 2 tablespoons

Garnish: *Lemon and chopped chives*

1. Combine the bread crumbs, pecans, and seasonings in a pie pan. Whisk the mustard and milk in another.
2. Dip the fillets first in the milk, then in the crumbs—pat them on. Refrigerate 15 minutes to set the coating.
3. Sauté the fillets over moderately high heat, using just enough oil to coat the bottom of the pan. Cook the fish 3 minutes on

3 tablespoons each: minced green onion and
  parsley
1 small red pepper, diced
Salt and pepper to taste

     1. Combine the chicken stock, 1 tablespoon of the oil, the carrot and the raisins in a small saucepan. Bring to a boil.

     2. Add the couscous and zucchini, stir. Place the peas on top of the couscous and set the pan aside, covered, 5 minutes.

     3. Uncover; fluff with a fork. Add the wine vinegar, remaining oil, and all other ingredients.

     4. Season to taste and let stand at room temperature 30 minutes to blend flavors. The salad is also good chilled.

MOROCCAN-STYLE FISH
Serves 4

4 thick fillets of firm fish (halibut, cod, or
  snapper)
About 2 tablespoons olive oil
1 medium onion, sliced
1/2 medium green pepper, seeded and sliced
1 carrot, peeled and sliced
1 jalapeño pepper, seeded and minced
1 clove garlic, minced
Salt and pepper to taste
Juice and minced rind of one small lemon
1 teaspoon ground cumin
3 tablespoons minced fresh cilantro
***Optional**: 1 tablespoon capers, rinsed and*
  drained
3 medium ripe tomatoes, peeled, seeded, and
  sliced

    1. Lightly sauté the onion in 1
tablespoon of the oil until golden; place it in a
casserole dish just large enough to hold the fish.
    2. Sauté the green pepper, carrot,
jalapeño, and garlic in the remaining oil until
soft; sprinkle over the onion.

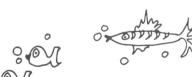

October

Melon or Pear Slices
with Prosciutto

Antipasto Salad

Mediterranean Pasta or
Pasta Primavera

Lemon Sherbet with
Raspberry Sauce

~ or ~

Turkey Saute with
Prosciutto and Sage

Spinach Timbales

Polenta

Apple-Cider Apples with
Glazed Pecans

Of course there is Pasta "Primavera" in the fall. It's an adaptable dish, quite good with most colorful, crunchy vegetables. Use the last tomatoes from the garden for the Mediterranean version; or try canned tomato wedges. Begin with crescents of melon or pear wrapped with thinly sliced prosciutto. An antipasto salad and a light dessert complete an authentic Italian dinner.

MEDITERRANEAN-STYLE PASTA
Serves 4

2 medium fresh tomatoes, or 6 to 8 plum
tomatoes
1 medium clove garlic, minced
1 tablespoon wine vinegar
2 tablespoons olive oil
1/2 cup marinated artichoke hearts, quartered
1/2 cup chopped black olives, preferably French
or Italian

Chopped fresh basil or oregano and parsley
    about 1/2 cup total
Salt and freshly ground pepper to taste
8 ounces pasta

1. Peel and seed the tomatoes; chop them coarsely to yield one generous cup. Save any juices and combine with all other ingredients except the pasta. Set the sauce aside.
    2. Cook the pasta in boiling salted water until al dente; drain and toss with the tomato sauce. Check the seasoning and serve the pasta immediately, or let it cool slightly and serve at room temperature.

Note: Good additions are fresh-roasted or canned sweet red peppers, chopped sun-dried tomatoes preserved in oil, and cubes of prosciutto ham. Toss with crumbled feta cheese, goat cheese, or Parmesan, if you wish.

Tip: When harvest is over and you need tomatoes, choose the plum variety. They're closest to that good summer flavor. —S.F.

PASTA PRIMAVERA
Serves 4

8 ounces fresh mushrooms
2 tablespoons butter
1 tablespoon each: lemon juice and water
1 cup broccoli florets
1/2 cup carrots cut into matchstick pieces
1/2 cup frozen peas
6 tablespoons cream cheese, at room
*   temperature*
1/2 cup (or more) freshly grated Parmesan
*   cheese*
8 ounces linguine or fettucine
1/4 cup minced green onion
Salt and pepper to taste
Pinch of freshly grated nutmeg
Minced parsley

1. Trim and clean the mushrooms; cut them into halves or quarters. Place them in a small saucepan with the butter, water, and lemon juice; cover and cook over high heat until they boil.

2. Drain the mushrooms and reserve the liquid. This technique keeps the mushrooms white and provides a sauce base.

3. Bring a large quantity of salted water to a boil. Cook each vegetable separately,

Note: These molds have the built-in garnish of bright green spinach leaves. They can be prepared and refrigerated several hours ahead. Or they may be baked ahead and reheated in a microwave.

POLENTA
Serves 4

2 cups water
1 cup yellow cornmeal
2 cups chicken stock
Salt to taste
2 tablespoons butter
1/2 cup grated Parmesan cheese

1. Stir the cornmeal into 1 cup of the water; whisk until smooth.
2. Bring the chicken stock and remaining 1 cup water to a simmer. Stir in the cornmeal and cook the mixture, stirring often, until thick, about 10 minutes.
3. Remove from heat and stir in the butter and Parmesan.

Note: The technique of blending the cornmeal with cool or room-temperature water before cooking helps avoid the lumps that plague polenta. Be sure to use a saucepan holding at least 1-1/2 quarts to control spattering.

APPLE-CIDER APPLES WITH GLAZED PECANS
Serves 4

Pecans
2/3 cup pecan halves
2 tablespoons each: sugar and honey
2 teaspoons pure vanilla
Cooking oil

Apples
1 pound tart apples (Jonathan or Granny Smith)
2 tablespoons butter
About 2 tablespoons sugar
1-1/2 cups cider
Optional: 2 tablespoons Calvados (apple brandy
~~~~~
Vanilla ice cream or frozen yogurt

1. Preheat the oven to 350° and oil two cookie sheets.
2. Combine the sugar and honey in a small saucepan and bring to a boil. When the sugar dissolves, remove from the heat and add the vanilla. Combine the sugar mixture with the pecans, coating them well.
3. Spread the nuts in single layer on one sheet, separating them, and bake them 8 minutes.

Immediately transfer them to the second sheet and let cool completely. Store air tight.

4. Peel, core, and slice the apples into even wedges about 1/2 inch thick.

5. Melt the butter in a large frying pan and add the apples, sprinkling them with sugar to taste.

6. Cook them over medium heat until soft and lightly browned, about 5 minutes.

7. Remove the apples; add the cider and the optional brandy to the pan. Boil rapidly until reduced by half. Return the apples to the pan, stirring to combine with the cider sauce.

8. Serve the warm apples and a few glazed pecans over ice cream.

There is no one who has cooked but has discovered that each particular dish depends for its rightness upon some little point which he is never told.

—Hillaire Belloc
English essayist

5. Fold the whites lightly into the chocolate, along with the vanilla and nuts. Fill the dish and bake 8 minutes; then reduce heat to 425° and bake a further 8 minutes, or until the soufflé is puffed and just set.

Note: The French way to serve a soufflé is with a slightly creamy center. Bake it a few minutes longer if you prefer it firmer. The soufflé is good with whipped cream or a vanilla custard sauce flavored with Frangelico (a hazelnut liqueur). Or simply sprinkle it with powdered sugar.

After a good dinner, one can forgive anybody, even one's own relations.

—Oscar Wilde
Irish poet and writer

December

Wild Rice Soup

Persimmon and
Spinach Salad

Pepper Steak

Browned Potato Balls
with Rosemary

Wine-Poached Pears

~ or ~

Christmas Eve Salad

Chicken in a Green
Almond Sauce

Calabacitas (Mexican-
style squash)

Kahlua Truffles

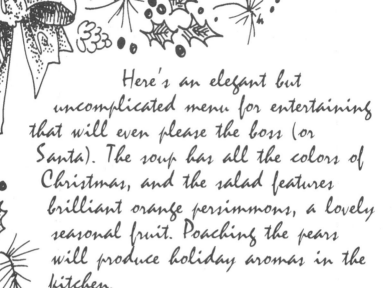

Here's an elegant but uncomplicated menu for entertaining that will even please the boss (or Santa). The soup has all the colors of Christmas, and the salad features brilliant orange persimmons, a lovely seasonal fruit. Poaching the pears will produce holiday aromas in the kitchen.

WILD RICE SOUP
Serves 4 to 6

2/3 cup wild rice
3 cups chicken stock
1 small green pepper, chopped
1/4 cup each: chopped red pepper, green onion,
  carrot, and celery
1/2 cup diced ham
1 cup mushrooms, cleaned and sliced
3 tablespoons butter
3 tablespoons flour
1 quart half and half
1 teaspoon thyme leaves
Salt and freshly ground pepper to taste

Optional but recommended: *4 tablespoons dry sherry*

Garnish: *A few chopped toasted almonds and some chopped parsley*

1.Wash the rice in cold water; drain. Bring the stock to a simmer and add the rice. Cover; cook over low heat until almost tender, about 40 minutes.

2. In a soup pot, sauté the vegetables and ham lightly in the butter. Sprinkle with the flour and cook 2 minutes, stirring.

3. Add the rice, half and half, and seasonings; simmer 15 minutes, or until the rice is cooked. Add the sherry and adjust the seasoning. Garnish and serve.

PERSIMMON AND SPINACH SALAD
Serves 4

Citrus Dressing *(Makes about 1/2 cup)*
2 tablespoons each: fresh orange and lemon
  juice
1 tablespoon honey, or to taste
1 teaspoon celery seeds
1 teaspoon very finely minced red onion
3 tablespoons oil
Salt and freshly ground pepper to taste

Salad
3 very ripe persimmons
2 ripe California avocadoes
1 small bunch spinach
1 head Belgian endive

1. Make the dressing by whisking all
ingredients together.
2. Peel the persimmons and completely
remove the core and the seeds. (The skin and
core are quite bitter.) Cut the persimmons and
avocadoes into crescents.
3. Wash and trim the spinach and
endive. To separate the endive, cut a cone shape
from the bottom and gently remove the leaves,
one at a time. Keep cutting the stem down to
remove the leaves intact.

4. Lay spinach leaves on each salad plate; fill in with some spears of endive. Lay the persimmons and avocadoes alternately over the top.

5. Drizzle with the citrus dressing.

persimmon

PEPPER STEAK
Serves 4

4 eight to ten-ounce fillet or strip steaks
4 teaspoons cracked black pepper
3 tablespoons oil
1 tablespoon butter
Salt
4 tablespoons each: dry vermouth (or dry white
    wine) and brandy
1 tablespoon Dijon mustard
1 large clove garlic
1 teaspoon tarragon
4 tablespoons cream or beef stock

Garnish: *Watercress or parsley*

1. Trim the steaks of all fat and press the pepper into both sides; coat lightly with 1 tablespoon of the oil. Let the meat rest half an hour at room temperature.

2. In a heavy skillet just large enough to hold the meat, heat the remaining oil and butter. Sauté over moderately high heat about 8 minutes for medium-rare, turning once. Salt the meat.

3. Skim excess fat from pan and flambé the meat with the brandy. Remove and keep warm.

4. Prepare the sauce by deglazing the pan with vermouth. Add the remaining ingredients and cook until blended and slightly thickened.

5. Pour the sauce over the steaks and serve with the watercress garnish.

BROWNED POTATO BALLS WITH ROSEMARY
Serves 4

1-1/2 pounds medium to large all-purpose
  potatoes
2 tablespoons butter
1 tablespoon oil
Salt and freshly ground pepper to taste
1 tablespoon minced fresh rosemary leaves, or
  1 teaspoon dried

1. Peel the potatoes and use a melon ball scoop to cut as many perfectly round balls as possible.
2. Place them in a saucepan and cover them with cold water; bring to the simmer and simmer about 5 minutes, or until they are barely tender. Drain the potatoes and pat them dry.
3. Over medium low heat, melt the butter and oil and add the potatoes, tossing them occasionally for 5 to 10 minutes, or until they are browned and fully cooked. Season to taste with salt, pepper and rosemary.

Note: Small, perfectly shaped vegetables have a certain elegance. There will be lots of wasted potato with this recipe, but just turn the scraps into some great potato-leek soup. The precooked potatoes can be patted dry and refrigerated for several hours before their final cooking.

WINE-POACHED PEARS
Serves 4

4 firm ripe winter pears—Bosc or Bartlett
1-1/2 cups dry red wine (Burgundy)
2 cinnamon sticks
6 whole cloves
1/3 cup sugar
2 strips of lemon or orange peel

1. In a saucepan just large enough to hold the pears, bring the wine, sugar, and flavorings to a simmer.

2. Peel the pears, leaving the stems on, and add them to the pan. Partially cover them and simmer, turning once, until just tender—10 to 15 minutes.

3. Let them cool in the liquid 20 minutes. Using a slotted spoon, remove the pears and rapidly boil down the liquid until syrupy and somewhat thickened.

4. Strain the wine syrup over the pears; cool and chill them.

Look South of the border for different fare on Christmas Eve. The colorful layered salad is full of seasonal fruits. Sauce for the chicken is a Mexican version of pesto—serve it with rice, adding chopped red pepper and green onion for a holiday touch. Unexpected seasonings give character to the squash, and truffle fans will love this version, a coffee and chocolate extravagance with a hint of orange.

CHRISTMAS EVE SALAD
Serves 6

Fruits and vegetables
1 small jícama, peeled and thinly sliced
4 small cooked beets, sliced
2 red apples, cored and sliced
1 small pineapple, peeled, cored and sliced
2 each: oranges and limes, peeled, seeded, and
   sliced
1 small bunch romaine, cleaned and shredded

Dressing
1/2 cup orange juice
2 tablespoons sugar, or to taste
4 tablespoons oil
Salt and freshly ground pepper to taste

Garnish: *The seeds of one pomegranate; 1 ripe avocado, in slices*

1. Place the shredded romaine in the bottom of serving bowl and layer the fruits and vegetables on top, ending with the pomegranate and avocado. Refrigerate until serving time.
2. Whisk together the dressing ingredients.To serve, pour the dressing over the salad, and lift out each portion. Do not toss.

Note: If only M.F.K. Fisher had written about how to tackle a pomegranate instead of how to kill a wolf! Accept this challenge, as the bright, jewel-like pomegranate berries are an essential holiday garnish. Select a pomegranate that is firm and heavy for its size. Be sure to wear an apron or some clothing that is deep crimson, as the juice stains badly. Cut the fruit in half, and score the skin of each half once or twice.

Peel off the skin; underneath you will find clusters of seeds encased in a papery membrane. Each seed must be plucked from the core of the fruit, and all of the membrane discarded, as both are bitter. Discard any seeds that are soft or grayish. The pomegranate will keep in the refrigerator for several days once opened, or you can proceed diligently and remove all the berries at once. The seeds also keep several days in a covered container.

Tip: Look for color and texture in salad greens: Boston, pale and soft; romaine, dark and crunchy; radicchio, great fuchsia accent. —S.F.

CHICKEN IN A GREEN ALMOND SAUCE
Serves 4

Sauce
4 ounces blanched almonds
One 4-ounce can whole green chiles
1 clove garlic
1 small onion
1-1/2 cups each: parsley sprigs and coriander
  leaves
1 cup chicken stock
2 tablespoons oil

Chicken
4 boneless skinless chicken breast halves
Salt and pepper to taste
1 lime—1/2 sliced, and 1/2 as juice

1. Toast the almonds at 350° for 8 minutes, or until very lightly browned.

2. Rinse the chiles and pat them dry. In a processor or blender, purée the sauce almonds, garlic, onion, chiles, and herbs until smooth.

3. Heat 1 tablespoon of the oil and cook the mixture, stirring, for 2 minutes; add the chicken stock and simmer 1 minute more.

4. Sauté the chicken breasts in the remaining oil until lightly browned, about 2 minutes per side. Season them lightly with salt and pepper.

5. Spoon the sauce into a baking pan just large enough for the chicken. Place the pieces

on top and bake at 350° about 15 minutes, or
until they are done.

6. Sprinkle the chicken with lime juice
and garnish with the slices.

CALABACITAS
(Mexican-style squash)
Serves 4

2 tablespoons oil
3 cups mixed zucchini and yellow squash, diced
1 clove garlic, minced
4 green onions, chopped
1 or 2 jalapeño peppers, seeded and chopped
1 cup frozen corn
Salt and pepper to taste
Pinch of cinnamon
1/3 cup each: chicken stock and cream
1/2 cup chopped cilantro

1. Heat the oil in a large frying pan, and
sauté all the vegetables about 5 minutes, or until
they are just tender.

2. Add the seasonings, stock, and cream;
simmer gently to blend the flavors. Sprinkle
with cilantro before serving.

Note: This dish can be made richer by
stirring in up to one cup of shredded Monterey
Jack cheese along with the seasonings and
cream.

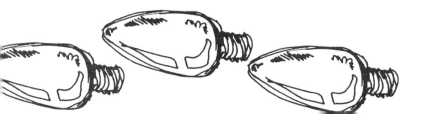

KAHLUA TRUFFLES
About 24

8 ounces best-quality semisweet chocolate, such
  as Lindt
1/2 cup whipping cream
2 teaspoons each: instant coffee and finely
  minced orange peel
2 tablespoons Kahlua (coffee liqueur)
About 3 tablespoons unsweetened cocoa
  powder

1. Finely chop the chocolate. Heat the cream with the coffee and orange peel until it boils; remove from the heat and stir in the chocolate until the mixture is completely smooth.

2. Add the Kahlua and refrigerate the chocolate about 2 hours, or until firm.

3. Sift the cocoa into a small plastic bag. Using a melon ball scoop , scrape the surface of the truffle mixture to form a rounded shape. Remove it with a toothpick, reshaping with your fingers if necessary.

4. Shake the truffles, two or three at a time, to coat them completely with the cocoa.

5. Store the truffles in the refrigerator, but bring them to room temperature about 15 minutes before serving.

Note: Another Mexican flavor is cinnamon—substitute 1/2 teaspoon for the orange peel if you wish.

The hostess must be like the duck—calm and unruffled on the surface, and paddling like hell underneath

—Anonymous

MY IDEAL KITCHEN

I am often asked for an opinion on various kitchen gadgets as well as on more substantial tools such as knives and cookware. Choosing knives, for instance, is a very personal thing—which one feels right in *your* hand, not mine, is critical. And your kitchen budget will also structure your choice.

Good sharp knives are essential so that you can cut quickly and efficiently while sparing your fingers. I believe you should buy the very best you can afford, even though it may take several years to complete a working set.

Which leads to the first item I wouldn't do without (after my Cuisinart): a Magnabar magnetic knife strip. I have two; one for small and one for large knives. These are wall-mounted near the preparation area. I can grab the right knife for the task without hassling with a knife block or (perish the thought) stabbing myself

while scrabbling through a drawer filled with
kitchen string and coupons as well as knives.

Another favorite, used almost every day, is
my Roto salad spinner. Centrifugal force produces
bone-dry salad greens without bruising even the
most fragile ones, and paper towels are left to do
what they do best—mopping up spills.

For finely puréed garlic, nothing is better
than the Susi garlic press. This Swiss-made model
is the best one I've found for thoroughly crushing
garlic cloves. When the clove is left unpeeled,
cleaning the press is a snap. Just use a toothpick to
pull out the skin before washing.

I relied on an instant-reading or bayonet
thermometer when I owned a restaurant. One
quickly learns in food service that the safe zone
for food is less than 45° and above 140°. The
thermometer lets you determine the temperature
in a matter of seconds. For the home cook, this
thermometer is no less useful—you know
immediately whether the roast is done or whether
the water temperature is right for adding yeast.

Whenever I cook pasta, I reach for my small kitchen scale. It tells me I have a two-ounce portion no matter what the shape of the pasta. It's also great for any recipe with metric measurements, or weighing out exact portions of meat.

Little helpers include pop-up sponges, which seem more durable than the supermarket variety, and my nutmeg grater, which brings the smell of Christmas to the kitchen. Whole spices retain their pungency much longer than the ground varieties, so I always try to use them.

Index

T

V

Z

the end